D1517073

Published in 2014 by The Rosen Publishing Group, Inc.
29 East 21st Street, New York, NY 10010

Copyright © 2014 Weldon Owen Pty Ltd. Originally published in 2011 by Discovery Communications, LLC

Original copyright © 2011 Discovery Communications, LLC. Discovery Education™ and the Discovery Education logo are trademarks of Discovery Communications, LLC, used under license. All rights reserved.

All rights reserved. No part of this book may be reproduced in any form without permission in writing from the publisher, except by a reviewer.

Photo Credits: **KEY** t=top; tl=top left; tr=top right; cl=center left; c=center; bl=bottom left; bc=bottom center; bg=background

CBT = Corbis; GI = Getty Images; iS = istockphoto.com; SH = Shutterstock; TPL = photolibrary.com

11t TPL; **19**tl SH; **24**bc, bl, cl iS; **25**bg iS; **28**bc GI; tr iS; c TPL; **29**bc CBT; bl iS; tl SH

All illustrations copyright Weldon Owen Pty Ltd

Weldon Owen Pty Ltd
Managing Director: Kay Scarlett
Creative Director: Sue Burk
Publisher: Helen Bateman
Senior Vice President, International Sales: Stuart Laurence
Vice President Sales North America: Ellen Towell
Administration Manager, International Sales: Kristine Ravn

Library of Congress Cataloging-in-Publication Data

McFadzean, Lesley.
 Ocean habitats / by Lesley McFadzean.
     pages cm. — (Discovery education: Habitats)
 Includes index.
 ISBN 978-1-4777-1322-8 (library binding) — ISBN 978-1-4777-1479-9 (paperback) — ISBN 978-1-4777-1480-5 (6-pack)
 1. Marine ecology—Juvenile literature. 2. Ocean—Juvenile literature. I. Title.
 QH541.5.S3M373 2014
 577.7—dc23
                                    2012043612

Manufactured in the United States of America

CPSIA Compliance Information: Batch #S13PK3: For Further Information contact Rosen Publishing, New York, New York at 1-800-237-9932

HABITATS

OCEAN HABITATS

LESLEY MCFADZEAN

LINDENHURST MEMORIAL LIBRARY
One Lee Avenue
Lindenhurst, New York 11757

New York

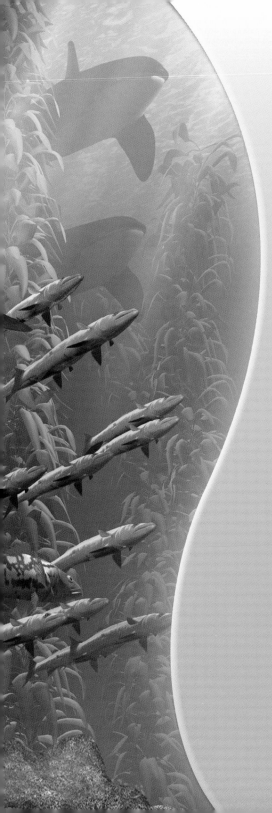

Contents

Five Oceans

Satellite photographs show Earth as a mainly blue planet because more than 70 percent of the planet is covered with water. Most of that water is in our oceans. Earth has five oceans but, since there are no physical barriers between them, the five meet and merge to form one large ocean. The International Hydrographic Organization defines where one ocean ends and another starts.

The largest ocean, the Pacific, covers one-third of Earth's surface, while the Southern Ocean around Antarctica, which was only officially recognized in 2000, is one-eighth the size of the Pacific.

Continents and oceans

The major oceans are bounded by continents. The Pacific stretches from the Americas west to Asia and Australia–Oceania; the Atlantic from the Americas east to Europe and Africa; and the Indian from Africa east to Asia and Australia–Oceania.

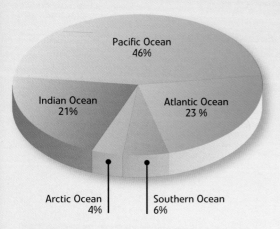

Pacific Ocean
46%

Indian Ocean
21%

Atlantic Ocean
23 %

Arctic Ocean
4%

Southern Ocean
6%

Ocean areas
The thee largest oceans—the Pacific, Atlantic, and Indian—make up 90 percent of the world's total ocean area.

NORTH
AMERICA

PACIFIC
OCEAN

SOUT
AMERI

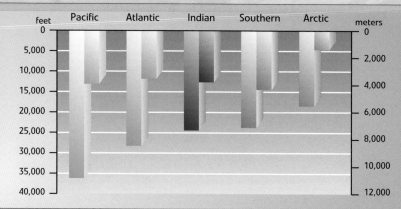

feet | Pacific | Atlantic | Indian | Southern | Arctic | meters
0 | | | | | | 0
5,000 | | | | | | 2,000
10,000 | | | | | | 4,000
15,000 | | | | | |
20,000 | | | | | | 6,000
25,000 | | | | | | 8,000
30,000 | | | | | |
35,000 | | | | | | 10,000
40,000 | | | | | | 12,000

OCEAN DEPTHS

Ocean floors are not flat, so two measures—maximum depth (longer bars) and average depth (shorter bars)—show ocean depths. The Southern Ocean is the deepest on average but Challenger Deep, near Guam in the Pacific Ocean, is the deepest point in the world's oceans.

Areas of ocean almost enclosed by land are called seas. For example, the Indian Ocean between Africa and the Arabian Peninsula is known as the Red Sea.

ARCTIC OCEAN

EUROPE

ASIA

AFRICA

Tropic of Cancer

Equator

LANTIC
CEAN

INDIAN
OCEAN

PACIFIC
OCEAN

Tropic of Capricorn

AUSTRALIA

SOUTHERN OCEAN

Antarctic Circle

ANTARCTICA

KEY
- ☐ Tropical
- ☐ Warm temperate
- ☐ Cold temperate
- ☐ Polar

Tides, Currents, and Waves

Oceans are restless because of the constant motion of tides, currents, and waves. The movement of tides, due to the gravity exerted on Earth by the Sun and Moon, is predictable because it occurs daily.

Most waves are created by wind on the water's surface, but there are also tall, slow-moving waves just beneath the surface. Wind generates ocean currents, and the major currents join together to make five large loops, or gyres. Because of the Coriolis effect (see below right), currents in the Northern Hemisphere turn clockwise, while those in the Southern Hemisphere turn counterclockwise.

Breaking waves
The bottom of the wave hits the seafloor, flattens, and slows. The crest breaks over the top.

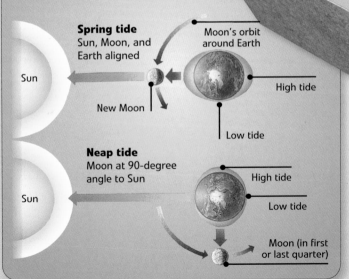

SUN, MOON, AND TIDES

The gravity exerted on oceans is greatest when the Moon, Sun, and Earth are aligned. This creates high, or spring, tides. When the Sun and Moon are at 90 degrees, the gravity exerted is weaker, and neap tides result.

Spring tide
Sun, Moon, and Earth aligned

Moon's orbit around Earth

Sun

High tide

New Moon

Low tide

Neap tide
Moon at 90-degree angle to Sun

High tide

Sun

Low tide

Moon (in first or last quarter)

Winds and waves

Most waves breaking on shore are created by wind on the surface of the ocean. The size of these waves depends on how strong the wind is and how far out to sea the onshore winds blow.

Wave dynamics
The water particles in a wave move up, over, down, and back, just like arms when swimming freestyle.

Crest

Trough

Wavelength
The distance between the crest (or trough) of this wave and the crest (or trough) of the next wave is the wavelength.

Wave height
The height, or amplitude, of a wave is the difference in height between the crest of a wave and the troughs on either side of it.

Coriolis effect

Wind

Gravity

The Coriolis effect
Gravity moves air between high- and low-pressure areas. Earth's rotation curves this moving air to the right in the Northern Hemisphere and to the left in the Southern Hemisphere.

Warm and Cold

Ocean surface temperatures range from a high of 69°F (20°C) to below freezing. The warmest tropical waters have an incredible diversity of plant and animal life, especially in winter when migrating animal species arrive. Temperate waters of the Northern and Southern Hemispheres are separated by the broad band of tropical waters of the three major oceans. The Arctic Ocean has permanent ice but the Southern Ocean freezes only in winter.

The Gulf Stream
Currents such as the Gulf Stream can affect the surface temperature of oceans by circulating warm water (indicated here as orange and yellow) from tropical to temperate zones.

Varied habitats

From freezing cold polar waters through to the warm waters of the tropics, there are ocean habitats suitable for every type of marine animal. Some make use of one habitat in summer and migrate to warmer waters in winter.

FROZEN OVER

An icebreaker is well designed to deal with polar oceans. Its broad hull provides stability in heavy seas and its steel-reinforced bow crushes ice in front of it. Animals are also well adapted to ice. Polar bears of the Arctic Ocean leap from one ice floe to another and penguins of the Southern Ocean belly flop, then slide across the ice.

An icebreaker crashes through ice.

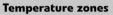

Temperature zones

Temperatures shown below
are for the top, sunlight zone
of oceans. At deeper levels, the
water temperature is colder.

KEY
- Tropical: more than 69°F (20°C)
- Temperate: 40–69°F (5–20°C)
- Polar: less than 40°F (5°C)

Polar oceans

In the Arctic summer, plankton
and krill provide food for
larger fish and mammals.
In winter, only fish with
"anti-freeze" chemicals in their
blood remain in the water.

Temperate oceans

Most of the fish we eat
come from the temperate
waters of the Atlantic
and Pacific oceans.

Tropical oceans

Coral reefs are the tropical rain
forests of the ocean, with
greater biodiversity than any
other ocean habitat.

Long Migrations

Long oceanic migrations are driven by the seasons and are all about food supply and the need to breed. Animals migrate with their own population along their own route, rarely overlapping with other populations, and use the same route year after year.

How do animals know their route? Birds use the Sun to orient themselves, whereas whales use Earth's magnetic field. Other migratory species may use smells and sounds to "recognize" the correct route.

Summer and winter
Humpback whales are marathon swimmers. They migrate between summer feeding grounds in cold waters, where they feed on schools of small fish and shrimplike krill, and their winter breeding grounds in warm tropical waters.

NORTH AMERICA
EUROPE
ASIA
AFRICA
SOUTH AMERICA
AUSTRALIA
ANTARCTICA

Arctic terns nest and breed in the Arctic summer.

Wingspans range from 29 to 33 inches (74–84 cm).

Longest migration
Arctic terns are the record breakers of bird migration. Large flocks fly from the Arctic to the Antarctic, a distance of 12,500 miles (20,000 km), then back again six months later. Most migrating birds break their journey to feed and sleep, but Arctic terns rarely do.

They feed on the move.

> *Humpback whales make a distinct sequence of noises that is called a song. The song changes according to the season.*

Humpback whales

Migration is very stressful for a humpback mother. Not only is she still suckling her recently born calf, but there is little suitable food along their migration route. She will lose weight before reaching the feeding ground.

Satellite transmitter fixed to the shell.

Signals beamed to satellite.

TURTLE TRACKING

Thanks to satellite tracking, we now know that loggerhead turtle hatchlings spend their first year in the Sargasso Sea, between North and South America, before taking advantage of the Gulf Stream to migrate to the Azores and Europe.

Data beamed to tracking station.

Computer picks up signal.

Scientist monitors data.

Sunlight to Darkness

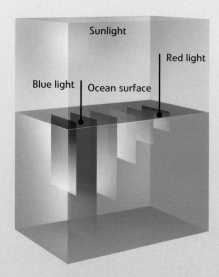

Sunlight

Red light

Blue light | Ocean surface

The ocean floor is an amazing landscape of high peaks, low valleys, and deep trenches. Between the floor and ocean surface are horizontal zones that are defined by the amount of light they receive. The most populated zone is the top 2 percent of the ocean, the sunlight zone. This is where sunlight penetrates, photosynthesis can occur, and where plants grow.

Microscopic algae, called phytoplankton, provide food for microscopic zooplankton and all the larger marine species in the food chain above them. Even where there is no sunlight—in the midnight and abyssal zones—there is life, some of it very odd.

The abyss

Below the midnight zone is the abyss, where gulper eel, sea spiders, blind shrimp, and tube worms live. In most parts of this zone, the only food is what falls from the zones above, except around the nutrient-rich smokers, or hydrothermal vents.

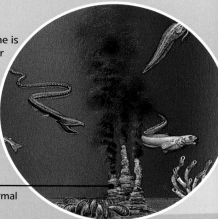

Hydrothermal vents

Light spectrum

Sunlight is made up of several colors, each with a different wavelength. Green and blue light travel deepest. Only blue light reaches the bottom of the sunlight zone and beyond. Below the twilight zone there is only darkness.

Undersea landscape

If the oceans were drained, a landscape of mountains, valleys, slopes, canyons or trenches, and plains would be revealed.

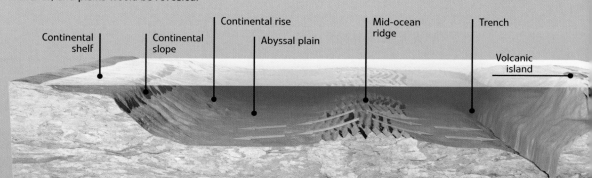

Continental rise

Abyssal plain

Mid-ocean ridge

Trench

Continental shelf

Continental slope

Volcanic island

Midnight zone
The large-mouthed, sharp-toothed fish in this zone are small because there is little to eat.

Twilight zone
Light here is limited but some of the fish are bioluminescent (emit light).

Sunlight zone
More species live in this plant-rich zone than in the other two put together.

Submarine ridge

Ocean zones

Oceans have three major horizontal levels or zones: the sunlight (euphotic) zone down to 660 feet (200 m); the twilight (disphotic) zone 660–3,000 feet (200–900 m), and the midnight (aphotic) zone, deeper than 3,000 feet (900 m).

Seawater in a bucket is colorless but the ocean appears blue because red, orange, and yellow light is absorbed and we see only the scattered blue light.

Ocean Shores

Ocean meets land in a variety of coastal environments: sandy or rocky shores, salt marshes, mangroves, sea grasses, and estuaries. Sandy shores are the most common, with three-quarters of the world's ice-free shorelines being sandy. The main problems on sandy shores are erosion and development, both of which affect marine life.

Rocky shores offer cracks, crevices, and intertidal pools as suitable habitats, but major storms can turn these upside down, exposing animals under rocks to predators and drying out.

Sandy shores
Shifting sands, constant pounding by waves, and few plants make sandy shores a harsh habitat. Many animals here are burrowers, and the main food sources are washed-up kelp, dead jellyfish, and phytoplankton.

Clams
These bivalve, or two-shelled, mollusks filter food from seawater.

The surface wash is sucked back.

Sand plover
This bird's short beak can only reach worms, insects, and small crustaceans near the surface of sand.

Burrowing
Large clams can burrow 3 feet (1 m) deep in sand to be safe from the drying sun, predators, and pounding waves.

Ghost crab
This small crab has a translucent shell flecked with yellow and pink that camouflages it in the sand.

Amphipod
There are 7,000 species of shrimplike amphipods, including sand fleas.

Incoming wave

Water filters back through sand.

Rocky shores
Animals that fasten onto rocks, such as limpets, and bendable plants are able to withstand wave shock at the surface. Farther below, wave shock is weaker and creatures are less exposed to drying air.

1 Barnacles
2 Limpets
3 Chitons
4 Blenny
5 Nudibranch
6 Mussels
7 Sculpin
8 Anemones
9 Starfish
10 Purple sea urchins
11 Hermit crab
12 Crab

TIDES

Since tides rise and fall twice a day, any marine plants and animals in the intertidal zone (between high and low tide) must survive out of water for up to six hours, although they do receive some water from spraying waves. Organisms below the tide line, in the subtidal zone, are permanently covered by water.

Subtidal zone

Intertidal zone

Rock pool

Intertidal zone

Splash zone

1 Sea hare
2 Giant kelp
3 Killer whale
4 Sea otter
5 Garibaldi
6 Ling cod
7 Sea urchins
8 Striped kelp fish
9 California barracudas
10 Kelp bass

Giant kelp grows up to 24 inches (60 cm) a day and is the world's fastest growing plant.

Shallow Waters

Coral reefs
A coral polyp secretes limestone to create an exoskeleton. As the polyp grows, it buds off new polyps that remain attached to it. Over time these coral colonies grow to enormous sizes. Coral reefs provide food and hiding places for many marine creatures.

I n temperate, shallow waters kelp, or brown algae, attaches itself to rocky reefs with a rootlike structure called a holdfast. Growing to a height of 165 feet (50 m), the tall kelp gets its nutrients from photosynthesis, just as trees do, and has a dense canopy, just like a forest.

Coral reefs are found in shallow, tropical waters to a depth of 33 feet (10 m). They are built from limestone secreted by tiny coral polyps and are the largest living structures on Earth. Microscopic algae, which require sunlight for photosynthesis, live within the polyp's tissue and are responsible for giving coral its bright colors.

9

10

Kelp forests
Some kelp species have a long, simple trunk, or thallus, with a frond growing out of the top. Other species, such as giant kelp, have fronds all the way up the thallus. Kelp, other algae, and plankton provide food for fish that, in turn, become food for larger predators.

TWO NUTRIENT SOURCES

Tentacles emerge from the coral's hard exoskeleton. When food touches a tentacle, it bends to bring food to the mouth, then down to the digestive cavity where enzymes break it down. Photosynthetic algae, called zooxanthellae, in the living tissue of the coral polyp also provide nutrients.

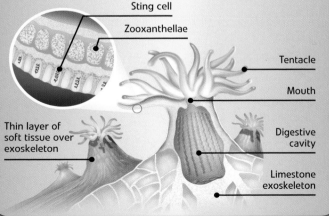

Sting cell

Zooxanthellae

Tentacle

Mouth

Thin layer of soft tissue over exoskeleton

Digestive cavity

Limestone exoskeleton

DARK AND DEEP

Below the sunlight zone, marine animals must adapt to depth and darkness. Some, like the lantern fish and deep-sea anglerfish, have light organs. The tripod fish uses its long fins and tail to "stand" on the ocean floor. The blue hake has exceptional hearing and the rattail fish has a great sense of smell.

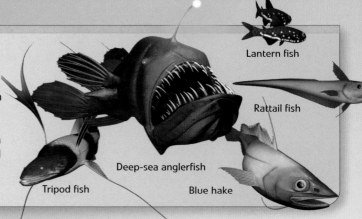

Lantern fish

Rattail fish

Deep-sea anglerfish

Tripod fish

Blue hake

Top or bottom

Oceanic species inhabit all levels of the ocean. Species that live in the top, sunlit layer are called pelagic species. Those that live on or near the seafloor are called benthic species.

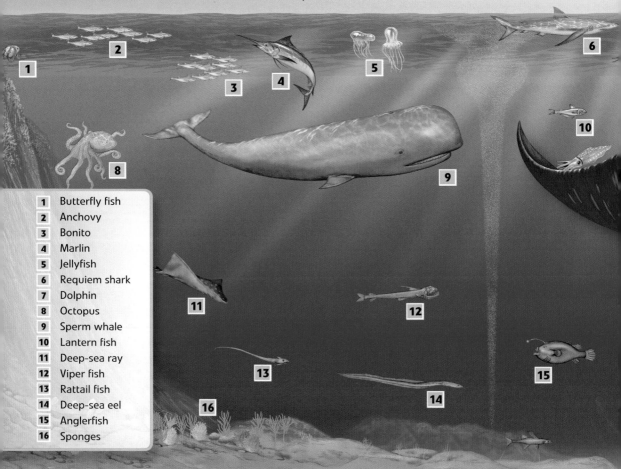

1	Butterfly fish
2	Anchovy
3	Bonito
4	Marlin
5	Jellyfish
6	Requiem shark
7	Dolphin
8	Octopus
9	Sperm whale
10	Lantern fish
11	Deep-sea ray
12	Viper fish
13	Rattail fish
14	Deep-sea eel
15	Anglerfish
16	Sponges

The Open Ocean

F ar from shore and shallow coastal waters is the open ocean. The marine animals living there are called oceanic species. The food chain for all these species rests on phytoplankton—single-celled algae that float near the ocean's surface—and zooplankton—tiny animal organisms.

Small species, such as anchovy, jellyfish, and lantern fish, eat plankton and are, in turn, eaten by larger fish, such as sharks or dolphins. Some species, including deep-sea eels and rattail fish, are scavengers that feed on dead organisms.

Smoker

Manta rays
These creatures grow to 22 feet (7 m) on a diet of drifting plankton. The two front fins direct the plankton into the ray's open mouth and the rear, or pectoral, fins are used for swimming.

7

Giant tube worms

Hydrothermal vents
These form over cracks in the seafloor. Superheated minerals spew upward and often form chimneylike smokers, which vent sulfur-rich water into the ocean. Giant tube worms convert sulfur into nutrients.

Crack in seafloor

Exploration

Only in the past 50 years have oceanographers had the technology and equipment needed to explore some of the world's ocean depths. This includes satellites in space that photograph the oceans, as well as unmanned vehicles, probes, and grabs that can be sent deep down where humans cannot go. Information from these observations is monitored and analyzed aboard vessels equipped as mobile research stations. The crew on these vessels control the movements of the unmanned observation tools, as well as retrieving the equipment or divers.

Sonar (sound navigation and ranging) technology has been used since 1913, but more recent equipment, such as the side-scan sonar and digital computer technology, allow for more accurate plotting of sonar data.

Underwater laboratory
Aquarius, the world's only undersea laboratory, lies 66 feet (20 m) below the surface, off the coast of Florida. A life-support buoy on the surface supplies air and power to the lab, which allows the aquanauts to return to *Aquarius* after a dive, taking their diving gear off in the special wet porch.

Sleeping area

Work area and kitchen

Entry lock and toilet

Wet porch

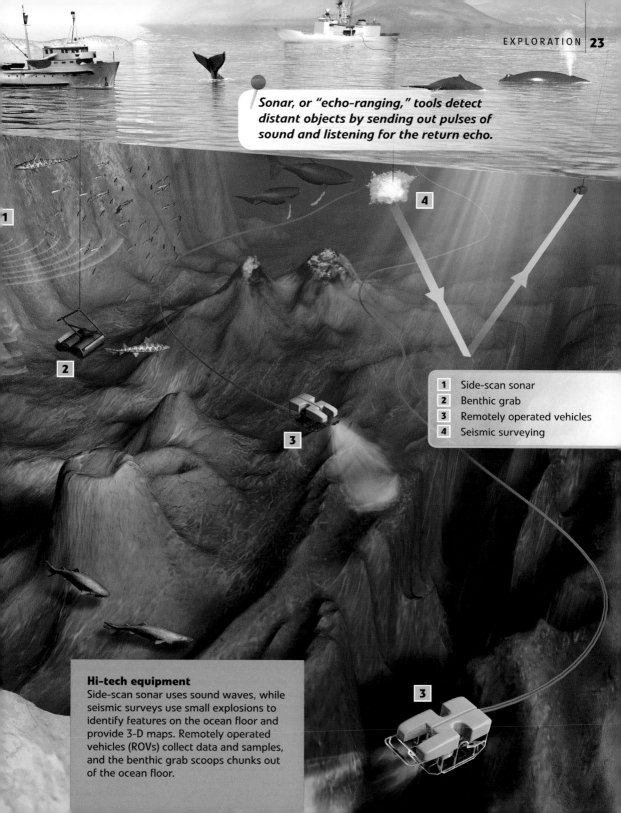

Sonar, or "echo-ranging," tools detect distant objects by sending out pulses of sound and listening for the return echo.

1	Side-scan sonar
2	Benthic grab
3	Remotely operated vehicles
4	Seismic surveying

Hi-tech equipment
Side-scan sonar uses sound waves, while seismic surveys use small explosions to identify features on the ocean floor and provide 3-D maps. Remotely operated vehicles (ROVs) collect data and samples, and the benthic grab scoops chunks out of the ocean floor.

Salts and minerals
Seawater is rich in salts and other minerals. Almost 90 percent of the dissolved salts is sodium chloride (table salt). The remainder is magnesium, potassium, and calcium. Most salt is extracted by mining salt beds.

Ocean Bounty

H arvesting the ocean is not as easy as harvesting or farming on land, but oceans could be just as bountiful. Oceans already provide fish and shellfish, oil and natural gas, salt and minerals, and kelp and seaweed, all of which we use in our everyday lives. There are also metals in the sea, marine creatures with medical properties, and alternative sources of energy.

If oceans are to provide us with resources into the future, we must consider the environmental impacts of our harvesting techniques and the sustainability of the resources.

Commercial fishing
Most of the world's commercial fisheries are in the temperate, coastal waters of the Atlantic and Pacific oceans. Stocks of some fish species are now seriously depleted through overfishing.

Sustainable energy
Producing energy from waves or tides is now possible. Aguçadoura Wave Farm, in the Atlantic Ocean near Portugal, is the world's first commercial wave-energy project. A tidal power station in France and two in Canada are forerunners of tidal-energy technology.

KELP PRODUCTS
The main substance extracted from kelp is agar. This is used as a stabilizer and thickener in food and other products. Agar comes from two species of red algae or kelp.

Toothpaste

Marine medicines
Research has revealed that a chemical from poisonous cone snails could produce strong painkillers. The toadfish, with its super-fast twitching muscles, may be useful in treating heart disease, and the horseshoe crab's blood is used to test for bacterial contamination.

Cone snail

Soap

Ice cream

Drilling beneath the oceans
Oil forms from dead plant and animal material that sinks to the bottom of the ocean, where it is trapped beneath layers of rock at high pressure and temperature. After locating the nonporous rock layer where the oil collects, an oil platform is erected at the site to drill down and pump up the "black gold."

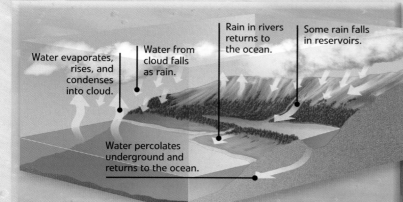

Water evaporates, rises, and condenses into cloud.

Water from cloud falls as rain.

Rain in rivers returns to the ocean.

Some rain falls in reservoirs.

Water percolates underground and returns to the ocean.

The water cycle
The Sun evaporates water in the ocean, the water vapor rises, and condenses to form a cloud. The cloud releases rain, known as precipitation, and the rain returns to the ocean via rivers, runoff, or underground percolation.

Oceans and Climate

Oceans play a major role in the amount of moisture in the atmosphere. Oceans absorb solar energy, release water vapor, which then condenses to form rain clouds, and the rainwater returns to the ocean in what is called the water cycle.

Oceans also absorb a large amount of the carbon dioxide from the atmosphere. In warmer ocean waters there is more evaporation, so more of the carbon dioxide is returned to the atmosphere, along with water vapor. In colder waters, more carbon dioxide is absorbed than released. Ocean temperatures, therefore, have a key role in reducing or accelerating the effects of climate change.

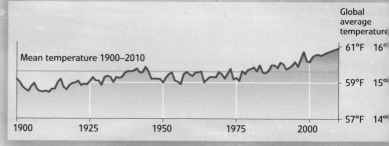

Global average temperature

Mean temperature 1900–2010

					61°F 16°
					59°F 15°
					57°F 14°
1900	1925	1950	1975	2000	

Climate change
Annual average temperatures (red line) have been visibly rising since 1900. In addition, since the late 1970s, average temperatures have always been above the mean temperature (yellow line) for the whole period.

An archive of data
Glaciologists drill through the Antarctic ice shelf, and the resulting ice core reveals the layers of ice and snow, year by year, which provide data about the chemistry and temperature of the water vapor in each annual layer.

Did You Know?

Do icebergs calve? Yes, they do. When an iceberg breaks off from the ice shelf and floats off into the ocean, this process is called "calving."

Threatened

Whether accidental or deliberate, human threats to marine life are growing. We not only pollute oceans with oil spills and garbage, but also with the carbon dioxide we emit. We have overfished to the extent that some fish species are critically endangered.

Since oceans border so many nations, international cooperation is needed to protect them. Closer monitoring of the seaworthiness of ships, limiting some forms of dragnet fishing, tackling pollution, and protecting areas of ocean in marine parks are some options for the future.

Coral bleaching and algae
Rising sea temperatures have bleached large areas of coral in the tropics, killing the zooxanthellae in coral polyps that give coral its color. With no competing zooxanthellae, algae invade the bleached coral and alter the food chain.

Oil spills
Leaking offshore oil drilling rigs and oil tankers that run aground and spill oil are disastrous for nearby marine life. In the time it takes to clean up the spill, thousands of oil-soaked birds, oxygen-breathing plants and animals, as well as fish and their eggs, can die.

Commercial fishing

Atlantic bluefin tuna, which can weigh 550 pounds (250 kg), swim near the ocean surface in large schools and are prime targets for commercial fishing boats. In the past 40 years, stocks have dropped by 80 percent and this species is now critically endangered.

Accidental catches

Many species of dolphins and sharks are caught and drowned accidentally in commercial fishing nets. These unwanted animals are called bycatch.

Choking garbage

A single piece of garbage can choke or strangle a marine animal. A large trash vortex, created by ocean currents and winds, makes areas of the Pacific and Atlantic oceans almost uninhabitable.

Glossary

abyss (uh-BIS) The deepest horizontal layer of the ocean, beneath the midnight zone. From the Greek word meaning" no bottom."

agar (AH-gur) A jellylike substance extracted from red seaweed and used as a thickener in food and other products.

algae (AL-jee) Simple organisms that grow in freshwater and seawater. They are related to plants but have no leaves or roots.

amphipod (AMP-fih-pod) A small crustacean, such as a shrimp, with a flattened body and two kinds of limbs.

aquanaut (AH-kwuh-nawt) A skilled worker who lives in an underwater installation and participates in scientific research.

benthic (BENT-thik) Describes plant or animal life that is found on the seafloor. The opposite of benthic is pelagic.

biodiversity (by-oh-dih-VER-sih-tee) The variation in plant and animal life found in a habitat. Formed from "biological diversity."

bioluminescent (by-oh-loo-muh-NEH-sent) Describes fish, insects, bacteria, and fungi that produce visible light in special organs.

bycatch (BY-kach) Marine animals caught by accident in fishing nets meant for other species. Dolphins and porpoises are common bycatch.

coral polyp (KOR-ul PAH-lip) The soft, hollow body of a coral animal, with an opening surrounded by tentacles at the top. Some produce hard exoskeletons that eventually form huge coral reefs.

Coriolis effect (kawr-ee-OH-luh eh-FEKT) The effect on winds and currents caused by Earth's rotation. Winds are bent toward the right in the Northern Hemisphere and to the left in the Southern Hemisphere.

current (KUR-ent) A mass of water in the ocean moving between areas of different temperature. Warm currents move away from the equator, while cool currents move from the poles.

estuaries (ES-choo-wer-eez) Coastal regions where rivers flow into the ocean, and freshwater mixes with salt water.

gyre (JYR) One of five large loops formed by a number of rotating ocean currents, often involving large wind movements.

hydrothermal vent (hy-droh-THER-mul VENT) A fissure on the seafloor, usually near active volcanic areas, where heated water escapes from Earth's crust.

intertidal zone (in-ter-TY-dul ZOHN) The area of a shore between high and low tide. Tidal pools often form in depressions in the intertidal zone of rocky shores.

kelp (KELP) Large brown seaweeds with leathery fronds. Some species form large underwater forests.

krill (KRIL) Small, shrimplike crustaceans that form large swarms and are food for marine animals such as squid, penguins, seals, and whales.

mangrove (MAN-grohv)
A tree or shrub that grows in shallow, often salty, water or mud in the tropics. Since they are rooted in water, mangroves have aerial roots to take in oxygen from the atmosphere.

midnight zone
(MID-nyt ZOHN) The black waters of the deep ocean below the twilight zone where sunlight cannot reach.

mollusk (MAH-lusk)
An animal with a soft body and no backbone, often enclosed in a shell. Limpets, oysters, mussels, and squid are mollusks.

neap tide (NEEP TYD)
A tide where the difference between low and high tide is small. It occurs when the Moon and Sun are at 90 degrees.

oceanic (uh-shee-A-nik)
Describes the open ocean far away from continents, as well as the species that live there.

organism
(OR-guh-nih-zum) An individual living thing—plant or animal.

overfish (oh-ver-FISH)
To catch so many fish that the population of that species cannot reproduce enough young fish to replace themselves.

pelagic (puh-LAY-jik)
Describes plants and animals that inhabit the upper, sunlight zones of the open ocean. The opposite of pelagic is benthic.

photosynthesis
(foh-toh-SIN-thuh-sus) The production of food by green plants, including algae and some bacteria. Sunlight provides the energy for photosynthesis.

phytoplankton
(fy-toh-PLANK-tun) Microscopic plants that produce their own food through photosynthesis. They are at the bottom of the ocean food chain.

population
(pop-yoo-LAY-shun) A group of animals of the same species that interbreed, live in the same place at the same time, and migrate together.

precipitation
(preh-sih-pih-TAY-shun) Water, in any form (rain, snow, hail, or sleet), that falls from a rain cloud to Earth's surface.

salt bed
(SAWLT BED) A layer of salt, often hundreds of feet thick and covering a large area, formed when past oceans receded, isolating some seawater that evaporated on land.

seismic surveying
(SYZ-mik sur-VAY-ing) A method of exploring the seafloor using strong, low-frequency sound waves.

sonar
(SOH-nahr) Short for "sound navigation and ranging," the technique of sending sound waves in water and measuring the distance to various objects based on the time it takes for the echo of the sound to return.

subtidal zone
(SUB-ty-dul ZOHN) The area of the shore that is always covered by seawater, even at low tide.

Index

A
abyss 14
algae 14, 19, 21, 24, 28
Arctic Ocean 6, 10
Atlantic Ocean 6, 11, 24, 29

B
bioluminescent fish 15

C
climate 26
   change 26
currents 8, 10, 29

D
depths, ocean 7, 22

F
fishing 24, 28, 29
   bycatch 29
   overfishing 24

G
Gulf Stream 10, 13

I
Indian Ocean 6, 7

K
kelp 16, 18, 19, 24

M
migration 10, 12–13

O
oil 24, 25, 28

P
Pacific Ocean 6, 7, 11, 24, 29
photosynthesis 14, 19
plankton 11, 19, 21
   phytoplankton 14, 16, 21
   zooplankton 14, 21

S
shore 8, 16, 17, 21
   rocky 16, 17
   sandy 16
sonar 22, 23

T
temperatures, ocean 10–11, 26,
   27, 28
tides 8, 17, 24
   neap 8
   spring 8

W
water cycle 26
waves 8, 9, 16, 17, 24

Z
zones, light 14–15
   sunlight 11, 14, 15, 20
zones, tidal 17

Websites

Due to the changing nature of Internet links, PowerKids Press has developed an online list of websites related to the subject of this book. This site is updated regularly. Please use this link to access the list: www.powerkidslinks.com/disc/ocean/